D0948901

NETFLIX®:

How Reed Hastings Changed the Way We Watch Movies & TV

WIZARDS OF TECHNOLOGY

WIZARDS OF TECHNOLOGY

NETFLIX®:

How Reed Hastings Changed the Way We Watch Movies & TV

AURELIA JACKSON

Mason Crest

Mason Crest
450 Parkway Drive, Suite D
Broomall, PA 19008
www.masoncrest.com

Printed and bound in the USA.

First printing
9 8 7 6 5 4 3 2

Series ISBN: 978-1-4222-3178-4
ISBN: 978-1-4222-3184-5
ebook ISBN: 978-1-4222-8720-0

Library of Congress Cataloging-in-Publication Data

Jackson, Aurelia.
  Netflix : how Reed Hastings changed the way we watch movies & TV / Aurelia Jackson.
       pages cm. — (Wizards of technology)
  Includes index.
  Audience: Age 12+
  Audience: Grade 7 to 8.
   ISBN 978-1-4222-3184-5 (hardback) — ISBN 978-1-4222-3178-4 (series) — ISBN 978-1-4222-8720-0 (ebook) 1. Netflix (Firm)—Juvenile literature. 2. Hastings, Reed, 1960-—Juvenile literature. 3. Video rental services—Juvenile literature. 4. Video recordings industry—Juvenile literature. 5. Internet videos—Juvenile literature. 6. Streaming technology (Telecommunications)—Juvenile literature. I. Title.
  HD9697.V544N483 2014
  384.55'8—dc23
                                    2014012229

CONTENTS

KEY ICONS TO LOOK FOR:

Text-Dependent Questions: These questions send the reader back to the text for more careful attention to the evidence presented there.

Words to Understand: These words with their easy-to-understand definitions will increase the reader's understanding of the text, while building vocabulary skills.

Series Glossary of Key Terms: This back-of-the book glossary contains terminology used throughout this series. Words found here increase the reader's ability to read and comprehend higher-level books and articles in this field.

Research Projects: Readers are pointed toward areas of further inquiry connected to each chapter. Suggestions are provided for projects that encourage deeper research and analysis.

Sidebars: This boxed material within the main text allows readers to build knowledge, gain insights, explore possibilities, and broaden their perspectives by weaving together additional information to provide realistic and holistic perspectives.

Words to Understand

innovation: A new, better way of doing something.

profit: Money that you make after all expenses have been paid.

pioneer: One of the first people to do something new.

business model: A business's plan for how it will make money.

technology: Something invented by humans to make a job easier or to make something new possible.

diverse: Having many different types or a great variety.

intimidating: Scary or discouraging.

technical: Having to do with the skills needed to make something.

CEO: Chief executive officer—the person in charge of running a company.

mediocre: Not very good.

venture: A business that involves some risk, where the outcome isn't certain.

CHAPTER ONE

A Great Idea

Netflix had a big year in 2013. The online video rental company reached 40 million members and was still going strong. Getting to that point took a lot of planning, experience, and **innovation**. A man named Reed Hastings had seen a need in the world—and he invented a website to fill the hole created by that need.

Netflix began as a simple online DVD rental service that only stocked a few thousand titles. It was one of the first websites of its kind in a time when DVDs were not as common as other forms of media. The company did not make a **profit** for many years, even as its user base grew and grew. Yet Reed did not give up. He fought to expand the company because he believed Netflix would be a very important service in a

Reed Hastings has become one of the most successful people in the world of business on the Internet.

changing world. The rest of the world would realize Reed was right in just a few short years.

Reed Hastings was one of just a few people to *pioneer* online video rental. His *business model* was unlike anything else video rental services had ever seen. When *technology* changed, so did Reed. New features and possibilities were added to Netflix with the needs of the user in mind. Today, Netflix is one of the most popular online rental and streaming services, all thanks to one man's great idea.

REED'S YOUNGER LIFE

Successful business owners come from all walks of life, but they do have one thing in common: they know how to work hard! Reed started out with a very simple job. After all, he needed to get his experience somewhere. He began working as a door-to-door salesman, and what he sold wasn't at all related to movies. He sold vacuum cleaners!

Reed's occupation as a vacuum cleaner salesman began as a summer job. He originally planned to work for a few months before moving on to college. That all changed after he started the job and discovered that he really liked selling vacuum cleaners. College was put off for a year while Reed could learn how to be a better salesman. He spent an entire year selling Rainbow vacuum cleaners.

One of the ways Reed improved his skills as a salesman was by giving customers a first-hand demonstration of how the vacuum he was selling compared to the customer's vacuum. He did this by vacuuming the floor with a customer's vacuum, and then vacuuming the floor with a Rainbow vacuum. The difference between the two vacuums was so clear that Reed found it easy to make sales.

The next stop in Reed's early life was college. He moved to Maine and enrolled in a mathematics program at Bowdoin College. Mathematics caught Reed's attention because of how limitless the field was. There was always something new to learn, and he believed math was a great skill

Reed's time in Swaziland taught him a lot about himself and other people, all of which would help him become a successful businessperson.

to have because it could be use anywhere in life. Reed earned the Smyth Prize and the Hammond Prize before graduating from Bowdoin in 1983.

Reed enrolled in the military halfway through college because, he said later, he was "very interested in serving [his] country." He began training in the Marine Corps during the summer between semesters, but he did not like it one bit. Being a marine meant obeying orders without question, but Reed was always looking for ways to improve how something was done.

Reed also asked a lot of questions. "I found myself questioning how we packed our backpacks and how we made our beds," he explained in an interview. The Marine Corps was incredibly strict. Reed did not fit in. "My questioning wasn't particularly encouraged, and I realized I might be better off in the Peace Corps." Enrolling in the Peace Corps would allow Reed to help his country in a different way. He would also be free to ask as many questions as he wanted.

Reed did not waste any time joining the Peace Corps. He left for training on the day of his graduation from Bowdoin College. The Peace Corps is a volunteer organization that sends members to all areas of the world to help those in need. Peace Corps members can help by building houses, distributing food, or becoming teachers. The organization was a much better fit for Reed because it let him be who he was: a creative, inventive person.

Reed was sent to teach mathematics in Swaziland, a small country on the southeast tip of Africa. He lived far out in the country, away from any city. The school he worked in didn't even have electricity! Working for the Peace Corps taught Reed a lot about the *diverse* people in the world and their different needs. Everything he learned would prove to be useful later when he was building Netflix. He spent three years in Swaziland before returning home to the United States.

Reed's experience in the Peace Corps completely changed how he thought about the world and business. He didn't have much money while he was working for the Peace Corps, so he needed to learn how to live

Reed learned about computers at Stanford University, where many famous Silicon Valley entrepreneurs have gotten their start.

with very little. Sometimes, all he had was a meal and the clothes on his back. Later, he said, "Once you have hitchhiked across Africa with ten bucks in your pocket, starting a business doesn't seem too ***intimidating***."

Reed did not immediately start a business when he returned home to the United States. He chose to go further with his education instead, so he applied to Stanford University and moved to California to study computer science. Earning a master's degree is not easy, but the hard work helped prepare Reed for the future challenges of building his own company and keeping it strong. His understanding of computer science would help him build an online business.

FIRST COMPANY

All successful businessmen start small, and Reed was no exception. He worked at a small company known as Adaptive Technology after graduating from college. The company's main purpose was to debug computer software that wasn't working. Reed gained a lot of ***technical*** knowledge from the job, but some of his most important lessons came from people with far more experience than him.

One of the most important people Reed met at Adaptive Technology was Audrey MacLean, who was the ***CEO*** in 1990 when Reed worked there. "From her, I learned the value of focus. I learned it is better to do one product well than two products in a ***mediocre*** way," he explained. In other words, Audrey taught Reed to value quality over quantity. He learned that it's better to have a few great products than a lot of second-rate ones.

Reed worked at Adaptive Technology until 1991, when he decided to leave and start his own company. The first company he launched had nothing to do with movies. Before he started the company that would change how the world watched movies and television, he built another company known as Pure Software. The purpose of Pure Software was to find and fix bugs in computer software. The type of work Reed and his

Reed found himself struggling to manage so many employees at his first company.

employees did was very similar to what Adaptive Technology did, except on a much smaller scale. Reed Hastings' company could be hired whenever a computer program needed to be changed or just wasn't working right.

Pure Software took off very fast. Before Reed knew it, he was in charge of hundreds of employees. This growth was too much for Reed to handle alone. He was great at the technical part of his job, but he didn't know how to manage so many people. "As the company grew from 10 to 40 to 120 to 320 to 640 employees," he said, "I found I was definitely underwater and over my head."

Reed was overwhelmed by all the work that went into running a company. He sometimes wanted to give up ownership of the company and leave. "I tried to fire myself—twice," he said, but the board of his company would not let him quit. There was no choice but to stay and learn how to manage a large company. Reed did not give up, and he helped the company grow even larger and more powerful than before.

Pure Software hit a milestone in 1996, when the company announced it would merge with Atria Software, another software company. Atria specialized in creating powerful software, while Pure was best at fixing the errors in software. The two companies would make a great team. Reed was offered the chief technical officer (CTO) position at the new company in 1997, but he turned it down. He had learned a lot through Pure Software, and now he was ready to leave the company and do something new.

By the end of 1997, six years had gone by since Reed left his original job at Adaptive Technology, formed his first company, and then finally left that company in the hands of someone else. He had gained a lot of experience during that time, and now he planned to use that experience to start up a second, even more successful company. Reed wanted his next business *venture* to be more successful than his first, so he took his time thinking of the perfect idea.

Blockbuster Video was one of the most famous and successful movie rental businesses in the United States before Netflix changed the way people rent and watch movies.

That was when Reed came up with the idea for Netflix. At the time, video rental stores were very popular. DVDs were not widely used yet, so anyone who wanted to rent a movie would need to rent a videocassette tape at a store and bring it home to watch. Videocassette tapes are large, bulky, and heavy compared to DVDs. They are played using a VCR (a videocassette recorder). Most homes in 1997 used VCRs and videocassette tapes to watch movies.

Renting a movie in 1997 was very different from the way we rent movies today. Most video rentals took place in a store. There were a few popular video rental stores at the time. Three of the largest store chains were Blockbuster, Family Video, and Hollywood Video. All these stores followed the same business model; customers would enter the store, pick a movie, pay to rent that movie for a certain amount of days, and bring that movie home. It was up to a customer to return the movie before the due date. If she failed to do so, late fees were added to the movie price. A customer would be charged a certain amount of money for each day the movie was overdue. This was very inconvenient for people who misplaced the movie or simply forgot to return it before the due date. The fees could be very expensive.

Reed Hastings was one of the many people who used video rental stores in the 1990s. "I had a big late fee for *Apollo 13*," he recalled. "It was six weeks late and I owed the video store $40. I had misplaced the cassette. It was all my fault." At that price, it would have been cheaper to just buy the movie in the first place! Customers who are charged late fees are not allowed to rent another movie until they pay the late fees, so Reed had no choice but to pay the $40.

Reed was embarrassed and annoyed by the experience, which caused him to think of a better way to go about video rental. "On my way to the gym, I realized they had a much better business model," he said. "You could pay $30 or $40 a month and work out as little or as much as you wanted." A subscription-based video rental model would be like nothing else that existed at that time.

Text-Dependent Questions

1. What milestone did Netflix reach in 2013 and why is it important?
2. Why didn't Reed like the Marine Corps? Why did he move to the Peace Corps?
3. What important lesson did Reed learn from Audrey MacLean?
4. How was a customer punished if he returned a movie to the rental store past the due date?
5. What are the two ways Reed's new video rental company would be different from video rental stores?

Reed's new company would be different in another way, too. He would allow people to rent movies using an online service. Customers would not have to go to the store to pick up or return a movie because everything would be delivered straight to their door. An online rental service would be much easier for customers to use, and it would also be easier for Reed to manage.

Storefronts require a lot of money to run. A company needs to rent a building, hire employees, and pay money to keep the store running. An online service would require fewer employees and much less space, thus making the price of a rented movie much cheaper than a storefront rental store.

Reed also decided to switch to using DVDs as much as possible. DVDs are much smaller and lighter than videocassette tapes, so mailing a DVD would cost a lot less money than mailing a videocassette tape. Reed knew that Netflix would save both his customers and his company a lot of money by only offering DVDs for rent. He spent a lot of time perfecting

Research Project

Using the Internet, research video rental stores. Many of these stores declined and went out of business in the mid-2000s. How many video rental stores are still in business in the United States? Why do you think the other stores have been forced to shut down? What does Netflix have to do with the decline of video store rentals?

an envelope that would only cost just one first-class stamp to mail, making Netflix DVD rental cheaper than traditional video rental stores. Included in the envelope was a return envelope. It was very easy for customers to mail the DVD back.

With all these brand-new ideas in mind, Reed set to work and built his second company.

Words to Understand

early adopters: The first people to try out a new service or technology.

complexities: Complications; things that make a situation difficult.

revolutionized: Changed something in a big way.

queue: A line or a waiting list.

implemented: Made something; put into practice.

entrepreneur: Someone who starts a new business or takes risks in business.

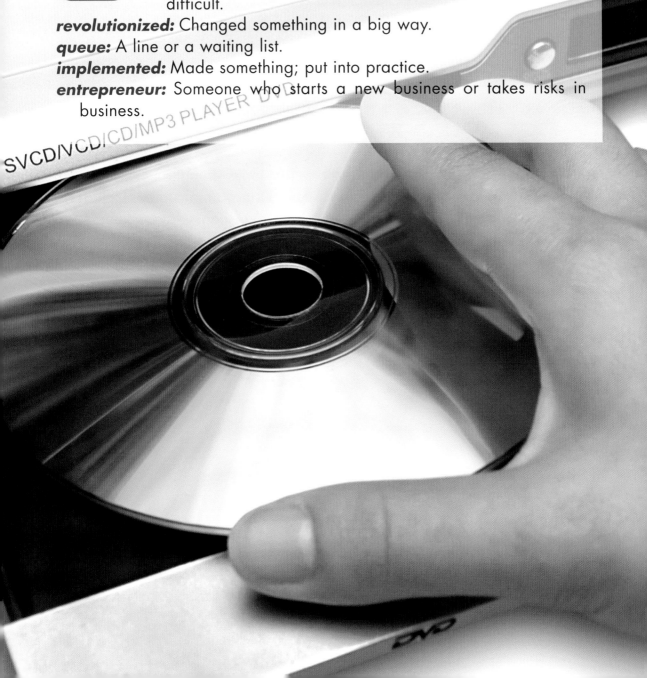

CHAPTER TWO

Changing Movie Rental

Netflix owes a lot of success to Reed Hastings and his ability to look to the future. Reed made a bold move when he decided Netflix would only rent DVDs and not VHS tapes. In an article titled "How I Did It" in *Inc. Magazine*, Reed explains, "It was still a dial-up, VHS world and most video stores didn't carry DVDs, so we were able to sign up **early adopters**. By the time there were enough DVD owners, we had gotten better and better and broadband had grown."

Netflix was one step ahead of video rental stores because the company started renting DVDs before anyone else. Videocassettes were the most popular way to view movies in 1997, and almost all movie stores only rented videocassette tapes. DVDs were still a new technology, and very few movies were released on DVD at the time. DVD players, which

Netflix's red envelopes for DVDs would become a famous trademark for the company.

were required to play DVDs, were also uncommon because of how expensive they were for people to buy. Reed knew it was only a matter of time, though, before DVDs were more affordable and more common than videocassette tapes. In time, the DVD player would go down in price, so Reed saw no reason to buy or stock videocassette tapes in his online store. By the time video stores started renting DVDs, Netflix would already have a huge selection in stock.

With a business model in place, Reed was ready to start his second company. He teamed up with Marc Randolph as his partner and got to work. The service was set up surprisingly quickly. Netflix was founded in 1997 and started offering rentals in 1998. Less than one thousand titles were available at launch, and the company had only about thirty employees. Each rental cost $4 per DVD, plus $2 for shipping. Netflix offered discount deals where a customer could pay less per DVD if more than one DVD was rented at once.

Reed thought his business would get a slow start because very few people owned DVD players, but he was wrong. Internet usage was just starting to boom, and paying for rental movies online was very convenient for people who owned DVD players. Netflix also allowed customers to buy DVDs directly from the website, which was something only a handful of online stores were doing at the time. All members needed to do after setting up a membership was put in their credit card information.

Netflix grew at an amazing rate. Once again, Reed found it hard to keep up with the expansion of his company. "Management was my biggest challenge," Reed admitted in *Inc. Magazine*. "Every year there were twice as many people and it was trial by fire. I was underprepared for the **complexities** and the personalities." Fortunately, Reed had Marc Randolph to help him manage the company.

In 1998, Reed made one of his very first tough business decisions. At the time, Netflix was both renting and selling DVDs. The company was spreading itself thin because it was focusing on too many areas of the

Netflix's incredibly large selection helped the company become popular with people who couldn't find their favorite movies at the local rental store.

Make Connections

Using Netflix was incredibly easy, which became one of its major selling points. Signing up on the website took just a few minutes, and linking a credit card to an account was just like paying for any other service on the Internet. A customer's billing information was saved for as long as the customer kept an account with Netflix. Picking a DVD could be done directly through the website, and it was usually shipped within the next day. The DVD arrived in a neat envelope, which could be opened and saved. When a customer was done with a DVD, all he or she needed to do was put the DVD back in the envelope provided by Netflix, and drop it in any mailbox. The next DVD in a customer's queue would arrive within the next few days.

DVD market. DVD rental was Netflix's most profitable area, which caused Reed to cease the sale of DVDs on the Netflix website. He thought back to what Audrey MacLean had taught him at Adaptive Technology: it was better to focus on one great product than a few mediocre ones.

Netflix was still growing. By 1999, the company had over a hundred employees and stocked over 250,000 DVDs. That's a huge jump from the original thirty employees and one thousand titles! Reed worked hard to make the newest, most popular movies available for rent the day they were released on DVD. Even with the amazing growth, Reed Hastings knew he had a long road ahead of him.

SUBSCRIPTIONS

When Netflix first began, ordering DVDs online wasn't all that different from renting a movie in a store. Customers still needed to pay a flat

Returning a DVD to Netflix is as easy as putting the red Netflix envelope in a mailbox, making the company's subscription a no-hassle way to rent movies.

Make Connections

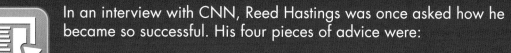

In an interview with CNN, Reed Hastings was once asked how he became so successful. His four pieces of advice were:

1. Target specific groups of people to use the service. Don't try to take on more than you can handle.
2. Stay flexible, and be ready to change your business plan if you need to. Netflix started out as a DVD mail rental business, but now its streaming option is one of the most popular features.
3. Never underestimate the competition. Competing companies may use a lot of time and resources to try to invent the next best thing. Stay ahead of them.
4. There are no shortcuts. Don't try to cut corners because it won't work. Not every company will be successful, and very few expand in just a matter of years.

rate to rent a DVD, and they still needed to return that DVD within a set amount of time. A customer who preferred picking up a movie at a store saw no reason to use Netflix, especially when video rental stores started carrying DVD rentals.

What Netflix did next completely **revolutionized** the movie rental industry. Reed thought back to his thoughts about his gym—and he decided his company was ready to move to a subscription fee plan. He explained, "Having unlimited due dates and no late fees has worked in a powerful way and now seems obvious, but at that time we had no idea if customers would even build and use an online *queue*."

There was no way to know if the subscription-based plan would work until it was **implemented**—but Reed was willing to take a risk. Netflix introduced a subscription-based plan in 1999. For the low price of $15.95

per month, customers could enter the Marquee Program. The new subscription program was as successful as Reed could have ever imagined. It was clear at this point that subscriptions were the next step in video rental.

Unlike previous rental options, the Marquee program had no late fees or due dates. Customers could preselect DVDs they wanted to see and place them in an ordered list, known as a queue. Only four DVDs were allowed in a queue at a time, forcing customers to visit the website and update their choices often. When one DVD was returned to Netflix, another DVD would be sent out automatically.

Customers did not need to return DVDs by a certain date. They were free to keep them for as long as they wanted, for a day or several months. Netflix did not care, as long as customers continued to pay for their subscription service. New customers were attracted to the new subscription-based model because no late fees meant no hassle.

By 2000, over 95 percent of users were subscribed to the Marquee Program. So many people were using the Marquee Program that Netflix saw no reason to continue selling the single-rental option. It was completely removed that year. Anyone who wanted to use Netflix would need to sign up for a monthly subscription. One of the reasons Netflix became so successful was its ability to adapt to the changing times, which included adapting to the changing demands of users.

SUGGESTIONS

There were a few ways Netflix stayed ahead of the competition. Offering DVD rental by mail was only the beginning of the website's expanding service. One of Netflix's more unique features was its ability to suggest movies based on what a customer had watched or rented in the past. Later on, customers were even able to rate films on a one-through-five scale. These ratings helped Netflix suggest new titles.

The suggestion feature was first added in 2000, but it was part of Reed's original business plan for Netflix. The feature became known as

CineMatch, with Cine being short for Cinema. CineMatch didn't just look at a customer's selections. It looked at what other users with similar tastes were watching and enjoying, too. A computer program was then used to predict what a customer would want to watch next.

Netflix continually tried to improve CineMatch. The company even hosted a contest challenging programmers to come up with a computer program that was better than the original CineMatch. Netflix offered a $1 million prize to anyone who came up with a better system. It didn't take long for a team to snag the prize, and that team introduced a program that improved Netflix's prediction rates by a little more than 10 percent.

Another feature of Netflix was the ability to add friends and see what they were watching. Social networking websites such as Facebook and Twitter were just starting to become popular. The friend system was Netflix's way to offer a similar function on its own website. Unfortunately, the friend feature was not very popular. Very few people used it, which lead to it being phased out completely in later years.

THE INTERNET BUBBLE BURST

New businesses require a lot of money to get started. It is common for most new businesses to not see a profit for several years. New business owners need to have enough money to make their companies last until they are profitable. Otherwise, the companies will fail before they ever make any money.

Netflix was first introduced in a time where plenty of Internet companies were just starting to rise in popularity. Very few websites existed in the early 1990s, and Reed was not the only *entrepreneur* to see an opportunity in building a website in the mid-1990s. The amount of online businesses trying to start up at one time meant there was a lot of competition between the newest websites. Companies that offered similar services to Netflix were forced to keep their prices low in order to keep customers and compete with the growing company. Most businesses simply

Research Project

Using the Internet, visit the "About Us" section of Netflix's website. How many employees does the company currently have, and how does that compare to the original thirty in 1997? How many subscribed users does Netflix have? How many users does the website have? Do you think the amount of users and employees will increase or decrease over the next ten years? Explain your reasoning.

did not have the financial backing to stay alive as the Internet expanded. If Reed wasn't careful, Netflix could be included in that group.

By the year 2000, it was clear that only a handful of online services would survive the turn of the century. "I didn't see the dot-com crash coming. It's hard to know when you're inside the bubble," Reed commented later. One magazine, *Barron*, predicted what came to be known as the Internet Bubble Burst before it happened. The magazine calculated that most start-up Internet companies would run out of money within the year. The only way to survive would be to start making a profit or seek the help of investors.

As successful as Netflix was, it was not making a profit yet. Reed Hastings and his company turned to investment firms for help. Investors are people who are willing to risk money by putting it into a company, in the hopes of making a profit in the future. People who invested in Netflix hoped to share some of the profit when the company began to soar. Investors are also given some say in how a company is run.

The money Netflix received from investors helped the company push through the Internet Bubble Burst. "We constantly invest in and improve our technology," Reed said. As more businesses failed, Netflix had an

Text-Dependent Questions

1. Explain why Netflix stopped selling DVDs.
2. How do free trials help a company gain more users?
3. Why was Netflix's new Marquee Service such a revolution in the movie rental industry?
4. What is CineMatch and how did it help users find movies they might be interested in?
5. What is the Internet Bubble Burst and how did Netflix survive it?

easier time succeeding because now it had less competition. Reed found ways to cut costs while still expanding the website's options. Netflix released a few new features over the next few years to solidify itself as a necessary service on the Internet. Reed was still thinking and still coming up with new ideas.

Words to Understand

regional: Serving a certain area.
distribution: The process of getting products from a business's warehouses out to customers.
stock: Shares of a company, which can be bought and sold.
evolve: Change over time.

CHAPTER THREE

New Ways
to Watch

Netflix's popularity was growing, but there was still one advantage video rental stores had over an online rental service: customers could enter a rental store and walk out with a DVD in just a few minutes. Meanwhile, Netflix users needed to wait several days to receive a DVD in the mail. "One mistake I made was waiting until 2002 to open *regional* warehouses for local *distribution* centers," Reed said later. Netflix might have grown at a faster rate had he opened local centers sooner.

The time it takes for a piece of mail to be delivered depends on how far away the mail is from the destination. A piece of mail that is sent from the same state will take a day or two to be delivered. Mailing a letter

Reed had to make sure subscribers were getting their DVDs in the mail in a timely way, making a trip to the video store seem like more work than walking to the mailbox.

from the East Coast of the United States to the West Coast could take up to a week. Local Netflix centers aimed at cutting down the delivery times to just one day.

The decision to open new centers was based on observations made by Reed's team. They noticed that there were more subscribed users in California than other states, and they thought the reason might be the distance from the data center. People in California would usually receive a DVD in a day or two, making them more likely to use this service. There were 5 percent more subscribers in San Francisco than any other area.

"Overnight delivery is so exciting to our customers and we were getting way too many complaints from subscribers that they had to wait too long," Reed said. For Reed and his company, the solution was clear: more warehouses would need to be opened so that customers could receive their rentals faster. "I learned from my mistake," Reed said. "We now have thirty-six warehouses spread out around the country."

Opening new buildings, hiring new employees to work at these buildings, and keeping the shelves stocked was not easy. It cost Netflix over $50,000 to open each new center, but the investment was well worth it. Customers were now receiving DVDs in record time, and new users were more likely to give Netflix a try because of how convenient it was.

Paying for all of these improvements was not cheap, and Netflix was still not making a profit. In fact, Netflix was about $14 million in debt. The money gained from investment firms was also not enough to keep the company going, even as Netflix's user base was growing. When the Netflix service reached 500,000 users in 2002, Reed knew it was time to take his company to the next level.

SETBACKS

Many companies face challenges, but one of the toughest is dealing with the competition. Netflix's success was no secret, and plenty of companies began to challenge Netflix by offering similar plans. Blockbuster, one of the largest traditional video rental store chains, started offering

Netflix's success hurt Blockbuster Video, causing the huge company's decline over the course of just a few years.

Walmart's DVD rental service caused some problems for Reed and Netflix, but Netflix was able to compete even with one of the largest companies in the world.

an unlimited subscription plan with no late fees. The plan was cheaper than Netflix's plan. It was unlike anything Blockbuster had ever offered before.

Walmart, a large superstore chain, also began renting DVDs with no late fees. This store became a threat because customers who shopped at Walmart went there for all sorts of items, including groceries, clothes, and electronics. It was very convenient for a shopper at Walmart to stop by the media section and check out DVDs to rent. Walmart removed the need to take a separate trip to a video rental store.

Netflix was quick to allow subscribers to rent Blu-rays, discs that hold more content and give users better picture and sound than DVDs.

Make Connections

Scientists work tirelessly to develop new technology every day. The transition from videocassette tapes to DVDs is just one example. Blu-ray discs were the next big advancement after DVDs. Blu-rays could hold more information and played movies at a much higher resolution. Home viewers could enjoy a picture crisper and clearer than ever before. Plus, more information could be stored in a Blu-ray than a DVD. The first Blu-ray discs were released in 2006, and Netflix began offering Blu-rays for rent soon after. However, the Blu-ray rental plan costs more money per month.

The competition Netflix faced caused the company's worth to drop. "When Walmart started a DVD subscription service in November of 2002, Netflix *stock* dropped to $2.50," Reed said. "I was surprised they entered the market, but I knew that they wouldn't be as focused as we are." Reed's answer to the pressure from Walmart was to open even more local centers, promising overnight delivery to plenty of large cities including Chicago, Dallas, and Portland.

The initial new centers were just the beginning for Reed. He imagined his business getting larger and stronger with each day. It would not be long until users from every area of the United States could receive a DVD in the least amount of time possible, but Reed did not want to stop there. He aimed to expand his business to reach all areas of the world.

These changes were what Netflix needed to succeed. The other companies could not compete with Netflix's selection, which only continued to grow with each month. No storefront could carry all of the DVDs Netflix did, and that collection grew with each passing day. Reed's plan worked, and the company began to succeed once more. For the

Video streaming changed the way Netflix did business, as well as how people surfed the Internet. Today, video is the most viewed type of content online (and Netflix is a big part of that).

competing companies, it was better to give up than to keep fighting. Walmart stopped offering rental services and instead returned to only selling DVDs. Blockbuster kept a loyal user base for a while, but it could not steal Netflix's customers.

Introducing Netflix Lite and adding even more local centers was exactly the change Netflix needed. The service experienced a boom in membership thanks to Reed's careful direction. At the end of 2002, the Netflix service had over 850,000 subscribers. This number jumped to 1,487,000 at the end of 2003. At this rate, Netflix would easily reach its goal of over 5,000,000 members by the end of 2009.

Netflix spent the next few years focusing on improving the service it already offered to its customers. One of the ways it did this was by updating CineMatch to be more accurate. Customers who rated the movies they watched would receive informed suggestions for future movies they might like. Netflix continued to increase its selection to accommodate the users' varying tastes. By 2005, the company held over 35,000 titles and was shipping 1,000,000 DVDs per day. The membership total also reached 4,200,000 people.

STREAMING

Netflix redefined movie and television-show rental by allowing users to rent DVDs online. Even though most users could now receive a rented DVD in a day, Reed knew the delivery of movies and television shows could still be faster. The speed of the Internet had improved greatly since Netflix first began, and watching a video online seemed like the next step in video rental. Reed became focused on introducing the next best way to rent videos, just like he had done with DVDs. This time, it was instant streaming. Streaming is another word for watching videos on the Internet, and it is instant.

Instant video rental may seem like new technology, but it is not. Plenty of cable companies have offered a similar service for a very long time. All users needed to do was select a movie on a television station and

Video on demand has become a major part of the movie and television business. From cable companies offering same-day rentals to Netflix's streaming service, there are more ways to get the movies and shows you love than ever before.

Text-Dependent Questions

1. How did Reed Hastings increase the speed at which users would receive DVDs?
2. How did Netflix overcome the competition it faced from Walmart?
3. Did Netflix invent the ability to stream videos and television shows instantly? Explain.
4. How did streaming help Netflix, users, and independent movie producers at the same time?

agree to pay for it. The fee for watching these movies could be paid instantly. Alternatively, users could pay by adding the fee to their cable bill.

The downside to the cable company's streaming service was that renting a movie was very expensive, and only a handful of movies were available at any one time. Older movies were usually not available for rent. Netflix, on the other hand, had so many movies that it would be impossible for one user to watch them all. Plus, a subscription to Netflix was cheaper.

In 2007, Netflix introduced the ability to stream videos. The user did not have to download the video or any additional software to see a streamed video. All he had to do was log on to the Netflix website to select the video by using the watch-now option. Unlike the cable on-demand service, Netflix users did not pay to watch each movie. The price was part of a larger package.

At first, streaming was offered in addition to physical DVD rental. Not all shows or movies were available online, so users were lucky if they found exactly what they wanted to watch. Over time, more movies and shows were added to those that could be streamed, and users of the website began watching streamed video more than physical DVDs. Netflix

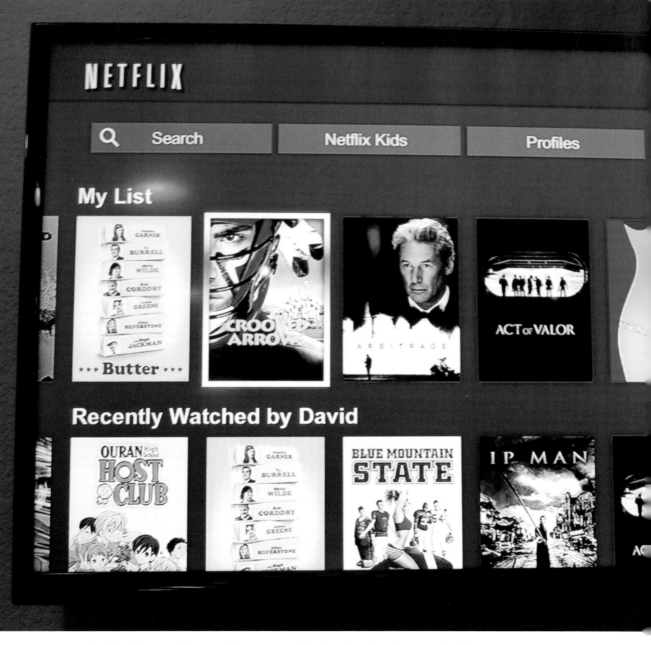

Netflix has been able to adapt to new kinds of technology and offer its service on a huge range of the latest devices, including televisions and video game consoles.

Research Project

Using the Internet, research the differences between physical DVDs and streamed videos. Explain the technology between each. What are the advantages and disadvantages of both? Why might some users prefer to rent physical DVDs while others choose to stream videos instead?

was quick to react to its users' changing needs, and it began offering a streaming-only plan in 2011.

Streaming worked out very well for Netflix because it cut down costs in several ways. The company did not have to pay for shipping if users watched the movie online instead. Employees didn't have to pack a DVD, either, so it saved the company lots of time. As more users used streaming, less DVDs needed to be stored at the local centers. Some centers could even be closed. Users hoped the cost of a Netflix subscription would drop because streaming was cheaper for the company.

"We're very focused on making the streaming service better and better," Reed said. "Over time, all video around the world is going to become Internet video where each person can choose what they want to watch."

Netflix wouldn't be the only company to benefit from the way streaming was changing the world. Streaming gave lesser-known movie producers an easy way to get their content out there without spending a lot of money.

Reed had done what he always planned on doing, right from the beginning. "We didn't name the company 'DVDs by Mail,'" he said. Reed always knew his company and the technology that supported it would *evolve* into something better.

Words to Understand

dominated: Had total control of.

licensed: Allowed to use or do something by giving a legal permit.

equitable: Fair for everyone involved.

enhance: Make better.

biotech: Using the life processes of living things for industrial purposes.

information technology: The study or use of computers to store and transmit information.

accountability: Responsibility for whatever happens, good or bad.

sectors: Areas of business.

acquired: Bought by another company.

persistence: Continuing to try, even when things aren't going well.

CHAPTER FOUR

The Future
of Videos

All great businessmen make mistakes. Reed Hastings made a very big mistake in 2007 when he announced that Netflix and its services would be split into two companies. Netflix would continue to offer streaming, while another company took over DVD rentals. The second company would be known as Qwikster. "We realized that streaming and DVD by mail are becoming two different businesses, with different cost structures, " he explained in a blog post. "We need to let each grow and operate independently."

How this change would affect users varied from user to user. A person who only streamed videos would end up paying less than they were paying in the long run. Someone who wanted to both rent DVDs and stream videos through Netflix would need to pay more. Users who enjoyed all

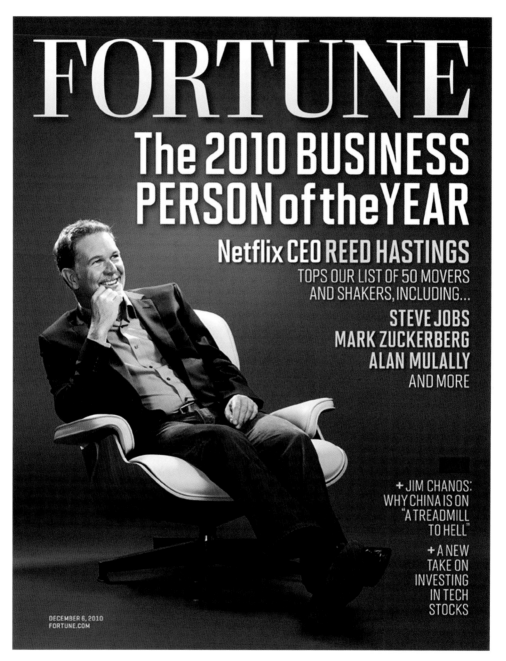

Reed has become one of the Internet's most successful businesspeople.

the benefits of Netflix were very upset about the change. Many of them threatened to leave Netflix completely.

"In hindsight, I slid into arrogance based upon past success," Reed admitted in an apology to Netflix users. He completely scrapped the plans to separate the services because of how much it upset the loyal customers of Netflix. Unfortunately, the lasting effect was that some users left Netflix and did not come back. The price of a Netflix share dropped by almost 70 percent. Over the next few years, Reed worked hard to win back his customers' loyalty.

The separation of DVD and streaming plans eventually went into effect, but the two plans did not become separate services. Instead, they were part of the same website and company. Streaming was unlimited, and users could pay extra to play videos on more than one device at once. DVD plans allowed a user to keep anywhere from one to four DVDs at once, with no due dates or cancellation fees. Blu-ray discs were also made available for extra money per month.

MORE COUNTRIES

By 2010, it was clear that Netflix *dominated* the video-rental market in the United States. One of the most popular rental stores, Hollywood Video, was forced to close that year. Blockbuster was also declining while Netflix membership continued to grow. Netflix saw an increase of membership by over 60 percent between 2009 and 2010.

With Netflix dominating the United States market, Reed began to look outward. Netflix's 20 million users made up only a small portion of the people in the entire world. Offering Netflix to other countries would help the company become even more profitable. The first country Reed chose was Canada. It was close to the United States, which meant DVDs could easily be mailed there.

Netflix launched in Canada in 2010. One year later, the service was offered to countries in Central and South America. By now, most of the

By 2011, Netflix had become one of the most important companies on the Internet, with millions of users spending hours watching videos every day.

With the rise of mobile devices like smartphones and tablet computers, Netflix has only become more popular. Now you can watch your favorite movie no matter where you are!

Western Hemisphere could use Netflix, and it was time to move on to Europe; 2012 was the year Netflix launched in the United Kingdom and Ireland. The service slowly began to expand around the globe.

Preparing Netflix for new countries takes a lot of work. More distribution centers need to be built because shipping from the United States to Europe could take a week or more. There are also some legal issues to worry about. Some videos are only *licensed* for certain countries, so not every movie or show is available to Europe, Canada, or South America.

Redbox allows customers to rent DVDs from vending machines for just one dollar. Netflix remains more popular, but Redbox may take business from Reed's company.

Make Connections

Netflix looks for quality in its employees. That's why the company chooses to pay employees more money than they would normally make at the same position at another company. "We're unafraid to pay high," Reed explains. Competition to work at Netflix is very fierce as a result, which means only the most talented and hard-working employees will stay at the job. The amount of time an employee is allowed to take off from work is also more flexible than at other companies, making Netflix a very desirable place to work.

Becoming an international company was new to Reed, but as usual, he has learned quickly. Netflix subscribers increased from 20 million to 40 million between 2010 and 2013. The membership count is expected to keep climbing for as long as expansion continues. Adding more countries to the Netflix coverage map will help membership to keep growing. The decline of DVD rentals and rise of streaming has helped make the move to being a global enterprise easier.

When asked if Netflix will one day be available in every country in the world, Reed replied, "It's something we certainly hope to do." According to him, the company should be able to provide service to all countries except China within ten years.

THE IMPORTANCE OF EDUCATION

Managing Netflix is not the only passion Reed Hastings has in life. In fact, he became very involved with education shortly after leaving his first company. "I was so ego-identified with Pure that I felt like a failure," he said. "After Pure Software, I had a bunch of money, and I didn't want

Reed believes that technology and education should go hand in hand. He hopes that bringing technology into schools can help solve many problems with education in the United States.

Make Connections

Reed Hastings currently lives in San Francisco with his wife and two children. He donates some of his money and time to help people get the same level of education he once did. Netflix is not the only company he has some sort of control over; he has been on the boards of Microsoft, Facebook, and nonprofit organizations throughout his career. He was once featured in an article in *USA Today* where he was pictured sitting on his Porsche car. According to him, he would like to have another picture of him taken, this time with him surrounded by a collection of movies!

to buy yachts and such things. I wanted to find something important to do."

According to Reed, "It's not a level playing field in K through 12 and we have to make it more *equitable* and successful to *enhance* what should be the strength of society, public education." He wondered why technology was increasing at such a fast rate, but the quality of education was still lacking. "There's great innovation in so many other areas—health care, *biotech*, *information technology*, movie-making. Why not education?" Reed believes all children deserve an equal education, and he wanted to help them get it.

Reed became a member of the California State Board of Education. He also donated millions of dollars to educational causes. According to his friend Nick McKeown, Reed is "absolutely driven to improve the level of education in this country." Unfortunately, Reed's opinions were not popular with everyone. After he suggested that there should be more English language testing for non-English-speaking students, he was denied the position of president of the board.

Netflix headquarters in Los Gatos, California.

Reed resigned from the Board of Education and focused his efforts elsewhere. He supports charter schools, which are unlike public schools in that they do not have to follow as many rules as public schools; they get public funding, but they operate independently. "If public schools don't adopt the same principles of competition and *accountability* as exist in the private and nonprofit *sectors*," Reed claimed, "they will continue to deteriorate."

Reed understands that not all Americans support charter schools, but he believes they can be very helpful "for students who don't get as much academic support at home." These schools can help children who fall through the cracks of standard education and need the extra help. Reed continues to use his money to support charter schools. He even donated over a million dollars to Beacon Educational Network to help open up more schools in his area.

REED'S FUTURE

Reed has no plans to leave or sell Netflix. "I have no need or desire to be *acquired*. We're making money, haven't used cash for three years, and have no problem with scale sufficiency." The company is very successful and will continue to be under Reed's guidance and leadership. He has certainly learned a lot since he first started managing people at Pure Software!

Text-Dependent Questions

1. What mistake did Reed make in 2007 and how did it affect the price of each Netflix share?
2. Netflix expanded to many countries starting in 2010. Why did Reed choose Canada as the first country where he expanded Netflix's service?
3. How long will it take before Netflix offers its services in all countries, excluding China?
4. Why did Reed decide to join the California Board of Education? What caused him to leave?
5. What are Reed's long-term goals?

Reed is still constantly learning. He explains that "being an entrepreneur is about patience and **persistence**, not the quick buck, and everything great is hard and takes a long time."

Making money isn't Reed's biggest goal in life. "If we can transform the movie biz by making it easier for people to discover movies they will love and for producers and directors to find the right audience through Netflix, and can transform public education through charter schools, that's enough for me," Reed told *Inc. Magazine*.

Netflix has opened the door to many new discoveries. And Reed Hastings has helped to change the world.

FIND OUT MORE

In Books

Belew, Shannon, and Joel Elad. *Starting an Online Business All-in-One for Dummies*. Hoboken, N.J.: Wiley, 2012.

Grinapol, Corinne. *Reed Hastings and Netflix*. New York: Rosen, 2013.

Keating, Gina. *Netflixed: The Epic Battle for America's Eyeballs*. New York: Portfolio/Penguin, 2012.

Lüsted, Marcia Amidon. *Netflix: The Company and Its Founders*. Minneapolis, Minn.: ABDO, 2013.

Selfridge, Benjamin, and Peter Selfridge. *A Kid's Guide to Creating Web Pages for Home and School*. Chicago, Ill.: Zephyr, 2004.

On the Internet

Funding Universe: Netflix, Inc. History
www.fundinguniverse.com/company-histories/netflix-inc-history

Inc.: How I Did It: Reed Hastings, Netflix
www.inc.com/magazine/20051201/qa-hastings.html

Netflix
www.netflix.com

The *New York Times*: Netflix Hits Milestone and Raises Its Sights
www.nytimes.com/2013/10/22/business/media/netflix-hits-subscriber-milestone-as-shares-soar.html?ref=netflixinc&_r=0

Wired: Netflix Everywhere: Sorry Cable, You're History
www.wired.com/techbiz/it/magazine/17-10/ff_netflix?currentPage=all

SERIES GLOSSARY OF KEY TERMS

application: A program that runs on a computer or smartphone. People often call these "apps."

bug: A problem with how a program runs.

byte: A unit of information stored on a computer. One byte is equal to eight digits of binary code—that's eight 1s or 0s.

cloud: Data and apps that are stored on the Internet instead of on your own computer or smartphone are said to be "in the cloud."

data: Information stored on a computer.

debug: Find the problems with an app or program and fix them.

device: Your computer, smartphone, or other piece of technology. Devices can often access the Internet and run apps.

digital: Having to do with computers or stored on a computer.

hardware: The physical part of a computer. The hardware is made up of the parts you can see and touch.

memory: Somewhere that a computer stores information that it is using.

media: Short for multimedia, it's the entertainment or information that can be stored on a computer. Examples of media include music, videos, and e-books.

network: More than one computer or device connected together so information can be shared between them.

pixel: A dot of light or color on a digital display. A computer monitor or phone screen has lots of pixels that work together to create an image.

program: A collection of computer code that does a job.

software: Programs that run on a computer.

technology: Something that people invent to make a job easier or do something new.

INDEX

ABOUT THE AUTHOR

Aurelia Jackson is a writer living and working in New York City. She has a passion for writing and a love of education, both of which she brings to all the work she does.

PICTURE CREDITS

Dreamstime.com:
6: Marcel De Grijs
10: Elzbieta Sekowska
12: Joseph Mercier
14: Jakub Jirsák
16: Lynn Watson
20: Chan Yee Kee
22: Brandon Alms
24: 55hasan
26: Susan Law Cain
32: Kirsty Pargeter
34: Macsim
36: Ewapix
37: Gary Arbach

38: Teetotum
40: Syda Productions
42: Tomasz Jabłoński
44: Mitchblatt
46: Marcel De Grijs
51: Marcel De Grijs
52: Luckydoor
54: Zimmytws

8: James Duncan Davidson/O'Reilly Media, Inc.
48: *Fortune Magazine*
50: *The Hollywood Reporter*
56: Coolcaesar at en.wikipedia